Toddler & Preschool

GAMES

Introduction

Toddler and preschool age children can be a handful....to say the least!

One of the best ways to manage long days at home with young children is to focus on play. There's no better way to play than with a game.

Play isn't just about having fun (although that's important too!). It also helps build confidence, learn, develop social and problem-solving skills and children use it to process their emotions. And playing together is a great way to build bonds and memories as a family.

It can be too easy to dismiss toddlers and preschool-age kids as being 'too young' for games, but it's not true!

It's just about using very simple and fun activities that suit their age and keep them engaged.

I was amazed when I started looking online that there were so few resources available to parents and caregivers of young children who want to play with their kids. That's how *Toddler and Preschool Games* came about.

I've been collecting and testing (on my own kids) games and activities for over a year to create this must-have resource. A book crammed with hours of fun that you can play one-on-one, as a family or in a group, such as a party setting.

A note on adapting games...

Games are only fun to children if they feel like they're within their capabilities. The end goal has to be attainable, otherwise they'll lose interest and get frustrated. This might even lead to them losing confidence.

All children are different, and you know yours best. When you play the games in this book, adapt them to work for your child.

This might be allowing more time or switching out words for shapes, as this suits their vocabulary better. It could also be giving them subtle hints along the way to help them out.

Missing from the tray

Number of Players: *2*
Great for Playing: *1-on-1 or as a family*
Equipment: *Teatowel and some household items*

Collect a handful of small household items (your child can help you do this). Lay them out on a coffee table or a table.

Give your child a minute to memorise everything that is there. Now cover it with a teatowel and, in secret, remove one of the items.

Ask your child what is missing and see if they can guess.

If they're finding it too hard, you can take items away so there are fewer to remember and can add more if it's too easy.

QUICK CHANGE

Number of Players: *2 or more*
Great for Playing: *1-on-1, as a family or with a group*
Equipment: *None*

Someone is first to be 'on'. They stand in front of the other players and slowly walk around on the spot so they've done a full circle.

The person leaves the room and changes something about their outfit. It could be turning a t-shirt inside out or pulling your socks up. Make the change easier for little kids and harder for older ones.

The person returns to the room and does another full circle on the spot. The other players have to guess what they've changed.

Next, a new person is 'on'.

ACTIVITY IDEA

ARCHAEOLOGICAL DIG

Equipment: *Toys, an old toothbrush and a tray*
Great for Playing: *1-on-1*

Gather a tray of plastic toys (plastic animals and dinosaurs work great for this). Hide them in a tray or washing-up bowl and cover them with either mud, sand, or a flour and oil mix.

Have a second tray with water and an old toothbrush.

Tell your child that they are on an archaeological dig and all the toys need to be found and cleaned.

Would you rather eat only bananas or only apples?

Would you rather be a cat or a dog?

Would you rather wear your shoes on your hands or your hat on your feet?

Would you rather go down a slide or jump on a trampoline?

Would you rather have spaghetti hair or jelly legs?

Would you rather ride a dragon or a unicorn?

Number of Players: *2 or more*
Great for Playing: *1-on-1, as a family or with a group*
Equipment: *None*

Everyone finds a space and lies down on the floor.

Next, you say, "Wake up_____" and choose an animal, for example ", Wake up lions."

Everyone must then pretend to be a lion until you say "go to sleep". Repeat the process with a different animal.

Finish the game by saying "Wake up kids".

Wake up!

ACTIVITY IDEA

TOY RESCUE

Equipment: *Toys and printer's tape*
Great for Playing: *1-on-1*

Using printer's tape, tape your child's toys to the wall and furniture.

Your child then needs to go into the room and 'rescue' all the toys.

Number of Players: *2 or more*
Equipment: *Flashlight*
Great for Playing: *1-on-1, as a family or with a group*

You should make this game more fun by setting out obstacles in the room, such as a chair, a coffee table, and a blanket that someone could hide under.

Turn all the lights off and draw the curtains.

The adult starts the game by being the lighthouse. They stand at one end of the room holding a turned-on flashlight at waist height.

The rest of the players start at the opposite end of the room. The lighthouse starts the game by slowly turning around. The other players must hide so that when the light reaches them, they can't be seen. When it's dark again, they can move to a new hiding place.

The goal is for the players to reach the lighthouse without being seen. If you are seen, you are out and have to return to the start (be lenient with young players!). After the game, switch roles.

LIGHTHOUSE

***Number of Players**: 2 or more*
***Great for Playing:** 1-on-1, as a family or with a group*
***Equipment**: Ball or small beanbag*

Players throw the ball or beanbag to each other. While they do this, they count down from 10, followed by a "Splat".

"10, 9, 8, 7, 6, 5, 4, 3, 2, 1, SPLAT!"

Whoever is holding the ball on "Splat" has lost.

You can make the game extra fun by having whoever is the person who gets out mime a dramatic splat!

10 Seconds Splat!

ACTIVITY IDEA

RACING CARS

***Equipment**: Toy cars and printer's tape*
***Great for Playing:** 1-on-1*

Using the printer's tape, mark out a racing track on the floor. You can make this as elaborate as you like. The track could go up the walls in places, under or over furniture. You can also create and decorate stations and buildings using old boxes.

Now use your toy cars to race around the track!

CROCODILE SWAMP

***Number of Players**: 4 or more*
***Equipment**: Newspaper*
***Great for Playing:** With a group*

Lay out one sheet of newspaper per player on the floor. Play some music and have everyone dance around the room. When the music stops, each player must quickly find a sheet to stand on – their only escape from the 'crocodile swamp'.

Nominate an adult to be the crocodile, patrolling the swamp to spot anyone who steps off their newspaper. If someone does, the crocodile can tap-snap at them, and they are out.

Start the music again, but this time fold the newspaper sheets in half. When the music stops, it becomes trickier to stay balanced. The crocodile can try to make players laugh or jump to knock them off.

Continue playing, folding the sheets smaller each round until everyone is out.

In Out

Number of Players: *3 or more*
Great for Playing: *as a family or with a group*
Equipment*: Printer's tape or rope*

Using the printer's tape or a rope, mark out a big circle on the floor. It needs to be big enough for everyone to be able to stand in.

Someone sits out of the game and is the leader. They call "in" or "out" in whatever order they like. For example, "out, out, in, out, in, in, in".

Players' feet must stay together at all times. When the leader says "in", players jump so they are in the circle. When the leader says "out", players jump so they are outside the circle.

If someone does the wrong thing, falls or takes too long, they are out.

The final winner will be the next leader.

INDOOR HOCKEY

Number of Players: 2 or more
Great for Playing: 1-on-1 or as a family
Equipment: Softball and broom or newspaper

Set up a goal in the living room - you can use 2 chairs to do this.

Use a broom (a child's broom is ideal) or a rolled-up newspaper taped together as a hockey stick.

Take turns scoring goals. If your child has got the hang of this, then you can make it a bit harder by having the other player try to stop them by kicking the ball away.

ACTIVITY IDEA

FLOAT OR SINK

***Equipment**: Bath or washing up bowl and items from around the house*
Great for Playing: *1-on-1*

Collect items from around the house that won't get damaged if they get wet (toothbrush, spatula, a sock, etc).

Now fill up a washing-up bowl with water (or you can use a bath).

Have your child guess if each item is going to float or sink, then get them to test it out to see if they guessed correctly.

Would You Rather?

Would you rather cuddle a panda or a penguin?

Would you rather dress up as a dinosaur or a robot?

Would you rather jump in puddles or roll in leaves?

Would you rather sing a song or do a dance?

Would you rather read one book or five books before bed?

Would you rather go to the pool or to the playground?

PARCEL SURPRISE

Number of Players: *3 or more*
Great for Playing: *as a family*
Equipment: *Paper and newspaper*

Players collect items from around the house in secret. If your child is 3 or under, it will probably work best if they pair up with an adult to do this.

Next, using an old newspaper, wrap up your items.

Take your wrapped-up items to the other player to see if they can guess what's inside. They will do the same with you.

10 Seconds to...

Number of Players: *2 or more*
Great for Playing: *1-on-1, as a family or with a group*
Equipment: *None*

Say, "You have 10 seconds to.....", then state a task that your child must do. For example,
"....bring me something blue"
".....be standing on one leg"
"......bring me 3 things that are soft"

After the command, count down from 10 and see if your child can bring it to you in that time.

If you are playing with extra players, think of fun challenges that they must do together. For example,
"....be doing a piggyback ride"
"....both be standing off the floor"
"...be doing a dance together"

Don't forget to swap roles so your kid can also have a go at thinking up tasks!

LASER MAZE

***Equipment**: Printer's tape*
***Great for Playing:** 1-on-1, as a family or with a group*

In the corridor, set up a laser Maze. Do this by taping strips between the two walls. Make some high, some low and some diagonal.

Now challenge your child to go from one end of the corridor to the other without touching the tape, AKA, the lasers.

ACTIVITY IDEA

INDOOR CAMPING

***Equipment**: Blankets and cushions*
***Great for Playing:** 1-on-1 or as a family*

Use blankets, pillows, and furniture to create a cozy den in the living room.

You can use it to watch a film, read books or even bring your duvets and sleep there together overnight.

BLIND TASTE TEST

***Equipment**: Blindfold and food*
***Great for Playing:** 1-on-1 or as a family*

Blindfold your kid (you can get them to shut their eyes, but they'll probably cheat!).

Now feed them different foods - some yoghurt, a piece of apple, some bread.

Can they guess what they are eating?

If you are feeling brave, you can swap roles. Make it easier for them by laying out food options in advance on a plate, and then they can choose what to feed you.

ACTIVITY IDEA

ICE AGE

***Equipment**: Plastic toys, a bowl and a wooden spoon*
Great for Playing: *1-on-1*

In advance of this activity, take a handful of plastic toys (toy animals and dinosaurs are ideal). Put them in a plastic or wooden bowl with water and put it in the freezer overnight.

Remove the frozen mass from the freezer and give it to your toddler. Using a wooden spoon or a toy hammer, they can hit the ice to try to free the toys.

Follow the Leader

Number of Players: *4 or more*
Great for Playing: *with a group*
Equipment: *None*

One child is chosen as the leader.

The others follow any actions that the leader does. For example, if the leader jumps, everyone else jumps. Or if the leader touches their toes, everyone else must touch their toes.

The game can be played with everyone moving in a line of followers or with everyone in a circle.

Letter Game

Number of Players: *1 or 2 players*
Great for Playing: *1-on-1 or as a family*
Equipment: *Printer's tape*

This is a great game for practising letters!

Your child will need to be familiar with at least some letters of the alphabet. Using printer's tape, create letters on the floor that your child knows. Each letter should be big enough to stand on (or larger if you are playing with 2 children), and you can have as many as you like.

Next, give commands involving the letters, such as 'jump four times on letter T', 'Place a ball on letter B' or 'Turn around on letter S'.

Number of Players: _2 or more_
_Equipment__: Jigsaw puzzles_
Great for Playing: _1-on-1, as a family or with a group_

You'll need jigsaw puzzles that your child or children can complete.

Before the game starts, break up the puzzle and hide the pieces around the room.

On 'go', your child, or children if playing in a group, must find the pieces and then put them together. They keep going until the entire puzzle is complete.

PUZZLE SEEK

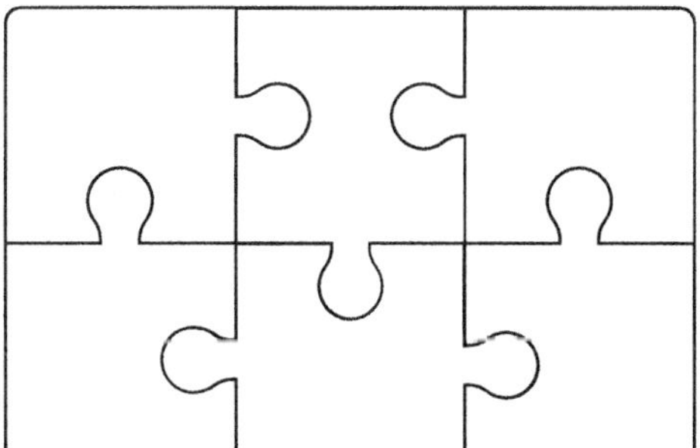

Keyword

Number of Players: *2 or more*
Great for Playing: *1-on-1, as a family or with a group*
Equipment*: None*

Ask your toddler or preschooler to pick a word. This will become your keyword.

Now start telling a story. If at any point you say the keyword, you close your eyes and start counting backwards from 10.

On 1, you open your eyes. In that time, everyone playing must have run and hidden somewhere so they are out of sight.

There are different ways you can play this game:
...Each time they hide, it has to be in a new place, so they can't keep just using the same spot.
....You can play this game throughout the day. So you can catch them out while at the shops or before bath time.
...You can mix up who is in charge of saying the keyword.

CHALLENGE

SHOPPING

***Equipment**: Vegetables and either a shopping basket or bag*
Great for Playing: *1-on-1 or as a family*

Give your child a shopping basket or a tote bag. You'll need a handful of hard vegetables (onion, carrots, potatoes, etc), or you can use toys if you prefer.

Get your child to turn around and then hide the vegetables in various places around the room. Your child must then go shopping and try to find all the items.

Now switch roles!

ACTIVITY IDEA

NIGHT HIKE

Equipment: *Flashlight*
Great for Playing: *1-on-1 or as a family*

Your little one will love the novelty of going on a night hike. This is perfect to do in winter when it gets dark early.

Get bathed and into pyjamas early. Now throw on coats and head somewhere exciting with your flashlights. A forest is ideal!

Let your kid wander, leading the way with their flashlight. Now turn them off and spend some time listening to the sounds of the night.

TOP TIP: Get hold of a UV flashlight from a second-hand site. Now you can search for bioluminescence in fungi and insects living in the woods.

Wrong Word Wrong Word

Number of Players: *2 or more*
Great for Playing: *1-on-1*
Equipment: *Books*

Grab a couple of your child's favourite books - they need to be very familiar with the story.

Read the book one page at a time. Tell your child that on each page, you are going to change a word. When they hear the wrong word, they have to say, 'wrong word, wrong word' and tell you the correct word.

For example, you might say 'The apple that came for tea' rather than 'The tiger who came for tea'.

A variation is to play this game with nursery rhymes instead: 'Twinkle twinkle little house'. For older children, they can also have a go at switching out words.

READY, STEADY, DRESS

***Equipment**: None*
***Great for Playing:** 1-on-1 or as a family*

This is a great game to play in the morning when you want to get out the house quickly.

Lay out your clothes on the floor and have a competition to see who can get dressed the fastest.

Variation:
If you want to make it more challenging, try getting dressed with your eyes shut!

Would you rather wear wellies or shoes?

Would you rather fly an airplane or drive a car?

Would you rather build a sandcastle or paint a picture?

Would you rather eat pizza or pasta?

Would you rather pull a silly face or be tickled?

ACTIVITY IDEA

THE FLOOR IS LAVA

Equipment: *Furniture and items around the house*
Great for Playing: *1-on-1, as a family or with a group*

Using chairs, tables, cushions and anything else you are happy to be climbed on, to create an obstacle course.

Can everyone get themselves from A to B without touching the floor? FYI, the floor is lava!

Add an extra layer to the game by continuing through different rooms. You can also encourage your child to create their own obstacle course and then test it together to see if it's possible.

DON'T LAUGH

***Equipment**: None*
***Great for Playing:** 1-on-1 or as a family*

Take it in turn to be 'on'.

The challenge is to try to get the person who is 'on' to laugh. The only rule Is you can't touch them, so no cheating with tickling! But daft dance moves, jokes and general silliness are all ok.

Once you succeed in making them laugh, swap roles.

Who is the best at keeping a straight face?

Number of Players: *3 or more*
***Equipment**: None*
Great for Playing: *1-on-1, as a family or with a group*

Grandma's Footsteps is a classic game where one player (Grandma) stands with their back to the others.

Everyone tries to sneak up on Grandma while her back is turned.

When Grandma turns around, anyone caught moving is sent back to the starting line.

The first person to touch Grandma without being seen moving wins and becomes the next Grandma.

GRANDMA'S FOOTSTEPS

Would You Rather?

Would you rather sneeze glitter or hiccup bubbles?

Would you rather roar like a lion or hiss like a snake?

Would you rather eat a cookie or a cake?

Would you rather live in a castle or a treehouse?

Would you rather swim like a fish or fly like a bird?

Would you rather ride a scooter or a bike?

Would you rather eat carrots or broccoli?

ONE WORD STORY

***Equipment**: None*
***Great for Playing:** 1-on-1 or as a family*

Someone starts the story with a generic word, for example, "I" or "the."

The next player will then say the next word, it can be any word at all as long as it makes sense in a sentence when added to the previous word/s.

The story continues with each player adding one word at a time.

If your child struggles with full sentences, you can just get them to fill in a gap. For example, 'The cat was very _____'

ACTIVITY IDEA

A TIGER FOR TEA

***Equipment**: Tea set and blanket*
***Great for Playing:** 1-on-1 or as a family*

Put down a blanket in the living room and have your child lay out a tea set. You can either do lunch for real or pretend.

Have them invite all their favourite teddies and dolls to join you.

You can make it extra fun by also having everyone dress up.

MUSICAL

Statues

Number of Players: *2 or more*
Great for Playing: *1-on-1, as a family or with a group*
Equipment: *Music*

Play all your favourite songs and have a dance party.

Press pause on the music. When this happens, everyone must freeze. If you catch anyone moving, they are out.

Let your child have a go at controlling the music and seeing if you can stay still when they stop it.

ACTIVITY IDEA

HOUSE OLYMPICS

***Equipment**: A soft ball, printer's tape and plastic cups*
***Great for Playing:** 1-on-1 or as a family*

Create a series of Olympic home sports.

This could include...
....throwing a soft ball into a bucket
.....marking out the printer's tape on the floor and having them balance and walk along it
.....stacking cups in a pyramid
.....balancing a book on their head and walking from one side of the room to the other
.....balancing on one leg for a minute

See if you can invent any new fun challenges together!

Would you rather have wings or a magic wand?

Would you rather wear a superhero cape or a princess crown?

Would you rather have a tail or big floppy ears?

Would you rather feed ducks or feed goats?

Would you rather be as tiny as a mouse or as tall as a giraffe?

Bug in a RUG!

Number of Players: *6 or more*
Equipment: *Blanket*
Great for Playing: *With a group*

The children all sit in a circle. Place a blanket in the middle of the circle like a rug.

One child is selected as the guesser and leaves the room. Choose another to hide under the blanket. Make sure everything is covered and instruct them not to move or make a sound.

The guessing child returns to the room and all the children sing, "bug in a rug, bug in a rug, come and see the bug in a rug." Now the guesser must try to work out who is under the rug.

Play again, but select new children to be the guesser and bug.

BATH FUN

***Equipment**: Duplo or pompoms*
***Great for Playing:** 1-on-1*

Bath play doesn't just need to be reserved for bedtime!

Fill up the bath and chuck in Duplo or a bag of pom poms.

Once finished, scoop the toys out and lay them out on a towel overnight or in the sun for a couple of hours so they are completely dry.

ACTIVITY IDEA

BOWLING

***Equipment**: soft ball and plastic cups*
***Great for Playing:** 1-on-1 or as a family*

Lay the plastic cups face down in a bowling ball formation.

Now take turns rolling the ball to see how many you can knock over.

You can make the game more challenging by moving the cups further away.

***Number of Players**: 2 or more*
***Equipment**: None*
***Great for Playing:** 1-on-1 or as a family*

Start by saying, 'I see with my little eye, something.....'. Then fill in the blank describing something you can see in the room. For example, 'something blue' or 'something big'.

When your little one has guessed what the item is correctly, switch so that they can choose something in the room that they can see.

I see with my little eye

Number of Players: *2 or more*
***Equipment**: Different coloured paper*
Great for Playing: *1-on-1, as a family or with a group*

Before the game starts, cut out different coloured circles, one for each player. So each player might have a blue, red, yellow and green circle, for example. The circles should be no bigger than the size of a plate.

Set a timer for 2 minutes for the first game; for future rounds, you can extend the time. Players must run around the house, collecting different coloured items that are the colour of the circle. Once they find an item, they must return it and place it on the corresponding circle. So if they find a blue book, it goes on the blue circle.

Players can only place one item at a time before collecting the next one. All items must be balanced in the circle; if they touch the floor, they don't count.

Once the timer is up, count the number of items. You get 1 point for each item, and the person with the most points wins.

COLOUR COLLECTION

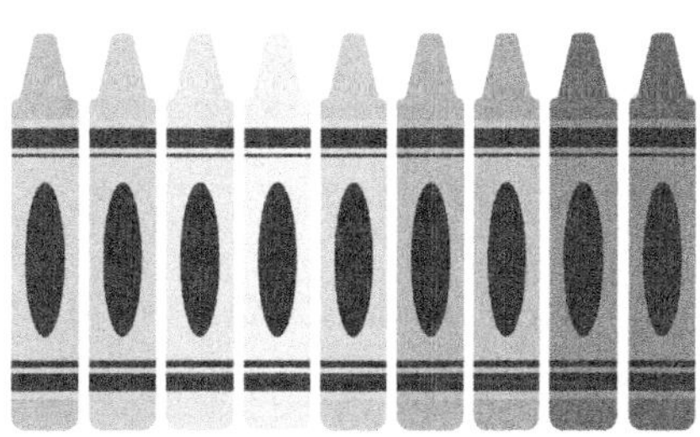

Odd One Out

Number of Players: *2 or more*
Great for Playing: *1-on-1, as a family or with a group*
Equipment*: None*

An adult should start the game. Begin by listing four things. Two of them belong together, and one is the odd one out. For example, "swing, slide, roundabout, car".

The other players have to guess what they think is the odd one out and why: "the car, because the other things are all playground activities". If you are playing in a group, players can put their hands up.

Whoever guesses first is then next to list items. If they are too young and will struggle, then you can stick to the adult listing items.

ACTIVITY IDEA

MUD BATH

Equipment: *Hot chocolate*
Great for Playing: *1-on-1*

Fill the bath partway and mix in a tub of hot chocolate to create a 'mud bath'. Throw in a few washable toys.

Your kid will love pretending they are bathing in mud. Once finished, drain the water and turn the shower head on to give them and the toys a wash!

Guess the Sound

Number of Players: *2 or more*
Great for Playing: *1-on-1, as a family or with a group*
Equipment: *None*

Have all the players sit at one end of the room with their eyes closed (also have them turn so they are facing the other way, as cheating is inevitable).

Find an item in the room that makes a sound - this could be opening and closing a drawer, shaking a tin of rice, pressing a doorbell, turning the tap on, etc.

The players must guess what the sound is. The first to guess right swaps with the leader and is next to make a sound with something.

Duck Duck Duck GOOSE!

Number of Players: *6 or more*
Equipment: *None*
Great for Playing: *With a group*

Have everyone sit in a circle.

Choose one child to be on. They walk around the circle, tapping each person on the head. As they do, they say "Duck" each time.

At any point, they can choose another player to be "Goose". When they tap their head and say this, that player must stand up and chase them around the circle.

They race to try to get back to the empty seat. Whoever gets there first sits down. The other player remains standing and continues tapping heads and saying “duck”, until they choose a new “goose”.

ACTIVITY IDEA

BUTTON LINES

Equipment: *Marker and card, coins or buttons*
Great for Playing: *1-on-1*

Take your marker and on a large piece of card, draw different shapes. For example a circle, swirl and square. You can do a more complex picture if your child is older.

Now give your child a bowl of coins or buttons. They need to line them up on the marker lines.

Once they've finished, turn over the piece of card. Now switch roles and get them to draw shapes or pictures, and you place the buttons or coins on the lines.

Hide & Seek

***Note**: If you have 3 or more players, you can try the Sardines variation*

***Number of Players:** 2 or more*

***Great for Playing:** 1-on-1 or as a family*

***Equipment:** None*

One person closes their eyes and counts to ten. Once they reach ten, they shout out, 'Ready or not, here I come.'

While they are counting, all the other players must run away and hide somewhere. Once the countdown is complete, the person must try to find the rest of the players. After everyone has been found, swap roles.

Your little ones will struggle with not peeking when they are counting, so you can get them to be in a different room.

SARDINES VARIATION

You'll need at least 3 players. This time, everyone waits in one room. One person goes off and hides somewhere in the house. The rest of the players then leave the room one at a time to try and find the hider.

Once they find them, they quietly join them (hence the Sardines name!). Last player to find everyone hiding is next to be on.

ACTIVITY IDEA

SOCK FIGHT

Equipment: *Socks*
Great for Playing: *1-on-1, as a family or with a group*

Have a sock fight!

Each person starts with a pile of socks. You can have a base, such as hiding behind a sofa or bed.

You'll want to set boundaries before starting, so you are only in rooms where things won't get knocked over.

Simon SAYS!

Number of Players: *2 or more*
Equipment: *None*
Great for Playing: *1-on-1, as a family or with a group*

One person is "Simon" and gives commands that the others must follow only if preceded by "Simon says." If they don't add this, then you shouldn't do the command - if you do, you are out.

For example, "Simon says jump as high as you can," and everyone jumps. But if they say "Turn around in a circle", then no one should do this.

Players can take turns to be Simon. You can also make the game harder by doing opposites. So if "Simon says stand up", everyone should sit down!

I'D JUST LIKE TO SAY........

Thank you for picking up a copy of *Toddler & Preschool Games* and making it to the end.

I tested every single activity and game out with my own children. It was great fun and helped strengthen my bond with them.....I really hope that's a gift that I am passing on to you!

It wasn't always easy, though. As any parent will know, it's a serious juggle managing any passion project alongside looking after small humans. But it has been worth the effort. Not just for the fun and games, but also because my children saw their mum pursuing her dream of being an author.

Before I leave you, I have a small (but very important!) favour to ask. As a teeny-tiny independent author, one of the biggest factors in how successful my book will be is the number of reviews I have.

It's mad, but true!

I'd therefore be *incredibly* grateful if you could take a minute, **right this moment**, and head to Amazon to leave this book a short review. I know you are busy and have a million things to do, so for anyone who does this, I want to say the biggest thank you!!

Please don't forget to also check out the other books in my series. If you love playing games, I've got you covered!! There's a reason my friends call me the 'games master'. I've published Family Games Night, Games for Couples, Party Games for Adults and more :)

Other books in the Games series....

And so many more!!

Printed in Dunstable, United Kingdom

70064473R00037